EYEWITNESS
SHAKESPEARE

Penguin
Random
House

Project editor Louise Pritchard
Art editor Jill Plank
Editor Annabel Blackledge
Assistant art editors Kate Adams, Yolanda Carter
Senior editor Monica Byles
Senior art editors Jane Tetzlaff, Clare Shedden
Category publisher Jayne Parsons
Senior managing art editor Jacquie Gulliver
Senior production controller Kate Oliver
Picture researcher Franziska Marking
Picture librarians Sally Hamilton, Rachel Hilford
DTP designers Matthew Ibbotson, Justine Eaton
Jacket designer Dean Price

RELAUNCH EDITION (DK UK)
Editor Ashwin Khurana
Managing editor Gareth Jones
Managing art editor Philip Letsu
Publisher Andrew Macintyre
Producer, pre-production Adam Stoneham
Senior producer Janis Griffith
Jacket editor Fleur Star
Publishing director Jonathan Metcalf
Associate publishing director Liz Wheeler
Art director Phil Ormerod

Special sales and custom publishing manager Michelle Baxter

RELAUNCH EDITION (DK INDIA)
Editor Ishani Nandi
Project art editor Deep Shikha Walia
Art editor Amit Varma
DTP designer Pawan Kumar
Senior DTP designer Harish Aggarwal
Managing editor Alka Thakur Hazarika
Managing art editor Romi Chakraborty
CTS manager Balwant Singh
Jacket designer Dhirendra Singh
Managing jacket editor Saloni Singh

This Eyewitness ® Guide has been conceived by
Dorling Kindersley Limited and Editions Gallimard

This abridged edition published in 2018
Revised edition published in 2015
Hardback edition first published in Great Britain in 2002 by
Dorling Kindersley Limited, 80 Strand, London WC2R ORL

Copyright © 2002, 2003, 2015 Dorling Kindersley Limited
A Penguin Random House Company
2 4 6 8 10 9 7 5 3 1
001–314163–Nov/2018

A CIP catalogue record for this book is available from the British Library.
ISBN 978-0-2413-8052-9
8-book set ISBN 978-0-2413-7902-8

Printed and bound in China

A WORLD OF IDEAS:
SEE ALL THERE IS TO KNOW

www.dk.com

CONTENTS

The early years

William Shakespeare was born in 1564, in the market town of Stratford-upon-Avon, England. His exact birth date is unknown, but it would have been shortly before his christening on 26 April. William was born into a wealthy middle-class family. His father, John, served on the town council and was one of Stratford's leading men. He worked as a glove-maker, and also dealt in wool and timber.

Shakespeare's birthplace
William was born in this house in Henley Street, Stratford. The house is now the Birthplace Museum and is furnished as it would have been in Shakespeare's day.

16th-century civic maces

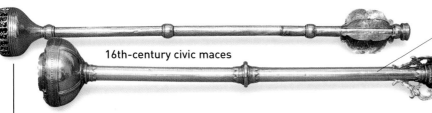

Maces were originally used as weapons

Blue dye came from the woad plant

Position of authority
In 1568, John Shakespeare was made high bailiff of Stratford, which was like being a mayor. His authority was symbolized by an ornamental staff called a mace.

Leftovers for sale
John Shakespeare bought sheepskins from the butchers to make his gloves. He cut away the sheep's wool, then sold it to Stratford's dyers and weavers. It was dyed using a variety of local plants and woven into cloth.

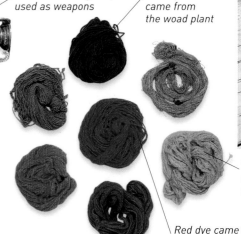

Yellow dye came from the weld plant, or "dyer's broom"

Red dye came from madder roots

16th-century velvet and satin mittens embroidered with flowers

Glove story
In the 16th century, wealthy people wore beautifully embroidered gloves like these mittens. John would not have sewn them himself. Embroidery was done mainly in the home by women.

Henley Street
John Shakespeare's workshop was located in his house in Henley Street. Here, he cut and sewed the animal skins into gloves.

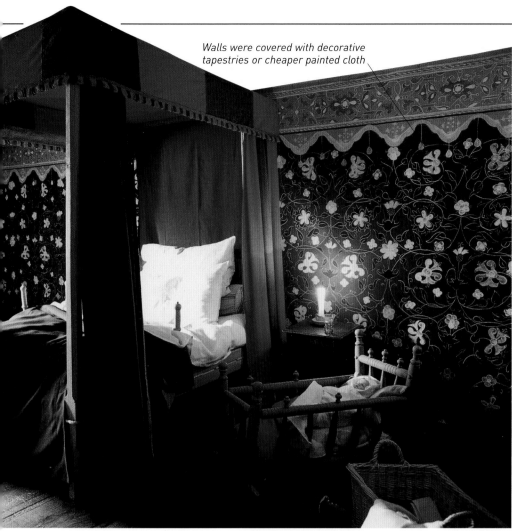

Walls were covered with decorative tapestries or cheaper painted cloth

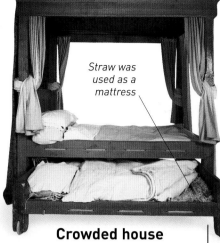

Straw was used as a mattress

Crowded house
William probably shared a "truckle bed" like this with some of his brothers and sisters. During the day, the lower bed could be wheeled under the upper one.

Mother's room
This is thought to be the room where John's wife Mary gave birth to William and his seven brothers and sisters. A cradle stands by the bed, and the basket is full of linen strips used to wrap babies.

Knobs and grooves carved by hand

Built to impress
As a small child, William probably sat in an elaborately carved high chair just like this. Parents who could afford such a fancy high chair would be seen to have wealth and good taste.

Family misfortunes
For a time, John Shakespeare's businesses were very successful, and he could afford expensive tableware like these pewter dishes. However, in 1576, when William was 12 years old, John got into debt and lost his position of importance in the town.

Going to school

At about the age of four, William Shakespeare would have gone to a "petty school" to learn to read. This was a small private school for boys and girls. At six, the girls left school to be taught at home, while middle-class boys like William went on to the local grammar school to learn Latin. At the time, people needed to know Latin if they wanted to follow a career in law, medicine, teaching, or the Church.

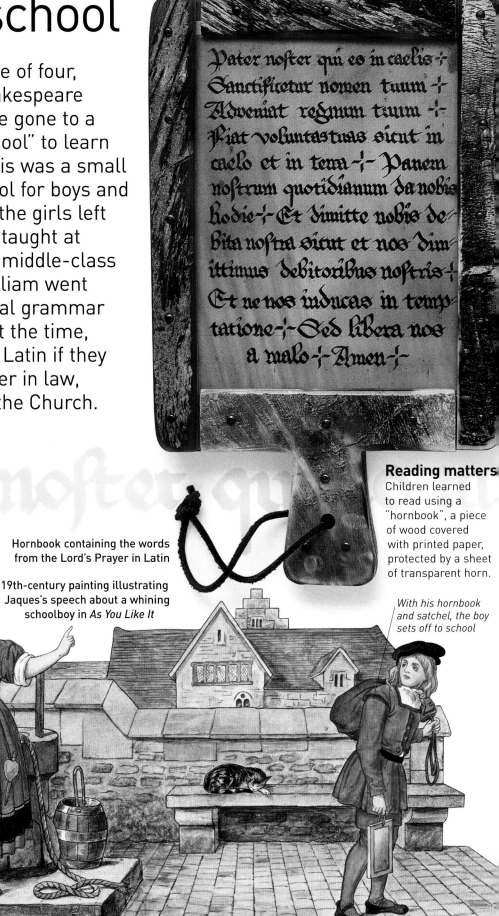

Birch twigs
Schoolmasters always carried a bundle of birch twigs. This was used to beat pupils when they misbehaved.

Pater noster qui es in caelis ÷ Sanctificetur nomen tuum ÷ Adveniat regnum tuum ÷ Fiat voluntas tuas sicut in caelo et in terra ÷ Panem nostrum quotidianum da nobis hodie ÷ Et dimitte nobis debita nostra sicut et nos dimittimus debitoribus nostris ÷ Et ne nos inducas in temptatione ÷ Sed libera nos a malo ÷ Amen ÷

Reading matters
Children learned to read using a "hornbook", a piece of wood covered with printed paper, protected by a sheet of transparent horn.

Hornbook containing the words from the Lord's Prayer in Latin

19th-century painting illustrating Jaques's speech about a whining schoolboy in *As You Like It*

Reluctant pupils
Most boys hated going to school. The hours were long, the lessons were dull, and their behaviour was strictly controlled.

With his hornbook and satchel, the boy sets off to school

Feathers tended to get in the way, but were sometimes left on for show

> "And then the whining schoolboy, with his satchel, and shining morning face, creeping like a snail unwillingly to school."

WILLIAM SHAKESPEARE
JAQUES IN *AS YOU LIKE IT*

The pen had to be dipped into the ink at regular intervals

Pen and ink
Pupils had to make themselves a pen called a quill from a goose feather. They cut the tip of the feather at an angle to make a nib. Ink was kept in an inkwell made of horn, wood, pottery, or metal.

Horn inkwells

selection of goose-feather quills

Balancing act
There were no desks, so pupils had to rest their work on their knees. This was no problem when they were reading from text books, but it must have been difficult when they had to practise their handwriting!

As he reads, the schoolboy follows the words with his finger

Tragic inspiration
At school, Shakespeare read the works of ancient Roman authors like Seneca, who wrote plays about suffering and death. One of Shakespeare's first plays was *Titus Andronicus*, a bloodthirsty tragedy inspired by Seneca.

Old favourite
One of Shakespeare's favourite writers was the poet Ovid (43 BCE–17 CE), whose poem *Metamorphoses* is a collection of stories drawn from ancient Greek and Roman myths.

5

The lost years

We know little of what Shakespeare did from the time he left school, at the age of 15, until 1592, when he was described as an up-and-coming playwright in London. Church records show that in November 1582, Shakespeare married Anne Hathaway. He was 18, while Anne was 26 and expecting their first child, Susanna. In 1585, twins arrived, who were named Judith and Hamnet.

Telling tales
According to one story, Shakespeare had to flee Stratford after being caught poaching deer. This story comes from Shakespeare's first biography, written in 1709 by John Rowe.

A place in heaven
One in three babies died in the 1500s. Christenings were important so that babies would go to heaven if they died. Susanna was baptized in Stratford on 26 May 1583.

Hathaway's house
William's wife Anne grew up in a large farmhouse in the village of Shottery, 2 km (1.2 miles) west of Stratford. Today, the farmhouse is known as Anne Hathaway's Cottage.

Father's footsteps
In Shakespeare's day, sons often followed their fathers into the family business. William may well have helped his father in the family wool-dealing business.

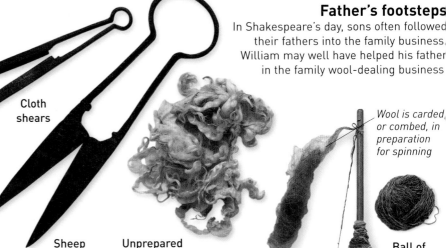

Cloth shears

Sheep shears

Unprepared sheep's wool

Wool is carded or combed, in preparation for spinning

Spindle, used to spin wool into a thread

Ball of thread

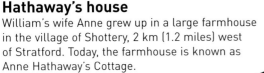

Hunting for clues

For hundreds of years, scholars have hunted for clues that might explain what Shakespeare was doing during his "lost years". His writing shows knowledge of types of work such as medicine, soldiering, and the law, which suggests that he may have had some personal experience of them.

Coneys, or rabbits

Wood pigeons

Goose

In the army
In the 1800s, scholar W J Thoms found a document naming a soldier called William Shakespeare. But this man was serving in 1605, when our Shakespeare was a successful playwright.

Medicine
Shakespeare's work shows that he had some knowledge of medicine, but his characters are often scornful of physicians, or doctors.

Elizabethan plates decorated with paintings and verses depicting professions

Staging a slaughter
Writer John Aubrey claimed that Shakespeare worked as a butcher, adding that when William killed a calf, "He would do it in a high style, and make a speech."

Spike to make holes for stitching

Half-moon shaped blade

Hooked leather knife

Leather-working tools

Green fingers
Shakespeare often mentions gardening activities, such as weeding, in his plays. This could mean that he was a gardener for a time.

Case closed
Shakespeare's plays are full of legal terms. In 1790, English scholar Edmund Malone suggested that the playwright gained this knowledge working in a legal office.

Leather working
Shakespeare is likely to have learned leather-working skills in his father's workshop. He would have used tools like these to make gloves, belts, or shoes.

16th-century engraving of Richard Tarlton

Taking to the stage
In the 1580s, several acting companies visited Stratford. England's leading company, the Queen's Men, performed in Stratford in 1587. William would surely have seen the company, and its star, Richard Tarlton. All we know for certain is that, at some point, Shakespeare became an actor.

Hand-coloured engraving of actors performing in an inn yard

Up to London

Apple-seller

In the 1580s, Shakespeare said goodbye to his family and set off to seek his fortune in London. He was just one of thousands of country people who moved to the great city in the late 16th century. On arriving, he would have been struck by the noise, dirt, and smells of the city. But he would have also been impressed by the beautiful churches and the grand mansions of the wealthy nobles.

A waterman was like a 16th-century taxi driver

Watermen worked either alone or in pairs

Crossing the river
Walking near the River Thames, Shakespeare would have heard the watermen calling out for passengers. The watermen rowed Londoners up and down the river, and across to Bankside and back.

A view of London from the south, by Dutch artist Claes Jans Visscher, c. 1616

Every day, thousands of people were rowed across the river to the playhouses at Bankside

Spreading city
When Shakespeare came to London, the city was spreading fast in all directions. Bankside, on the south bank, was rapidly becoming London's main entertainment centre.

Merchant and his wife, 1590

"Sack! Sack!" shouts a man selling wine

"Pen and ink!" cries a man selling quills

"Trinkets and toys!" calls the tinker

"Almanacs!" cries a man selling books

"Mackerel!" shouts a fishmonger

Sounds of the city

London was full of street sellers shouting out special cries to attract customers. Men and women wandered the streets, selling everything from vegetables, fish, wine, toys, and books, to quills and ink, fruit, brooms, pies, and second-hand clothes.

Merchants' might

The city was run by rich traders known as merchants. Trade was central to the wealth of the city, and every craft and trade had its own controlling organization called a guild.

Building up

Staple Inn (right), where wool was weighed and taxed in Shakespeare's time, is still standing today. As land was expensive, people built upwards.

The Latin text along the top of the map describes London as "The most famous market in the entire world"

The bells of more than 100 churches rang out across the city

TOTO ORBE CELEBERRIMUA

Shakespeare worshipped here, at St Mary Overie's Church, later known as Southwark Cathedral

Set of 16th-century standard weights

Traitors' heads were displayed on poles on London Bridge to warn the public against committing treason

Measure for measure

The guilds controlled trade using standard weights. Official measurers would check that members were not cheating their customers.

Queen Elizabeth I's court

When the Queen was not travelling the country, her court was based in the royal palaces around London. Elizabeth I surrounded herself with young male courtiers, who all competed for her favour. They flattered her by comparing her to the Roman moon goddess Diana, and called her "Gloriana", the glorious one.

Players at court
Elizabeth I never visited public playhouses. Instead, the players would perform private shows in the royal palaces. Shakespeare would have performed in front of the Queen before he became a playwright.

Pelican Queen
In this 1574 portrait, the 41-year-old Queen wears a pelican brooch. Female pelicans were thought to be perfect mothers, so the Queen wore this brooch to show how much she cared for her people.

White pearls symbolized the Queen's purity

Pelican brooch

Beauty secrets
The ladies at court used all sorts of lotions to try to remove spots or freckles. Herbs and spices were often used, but many of the recipes were harmful to health, or even poisonous.

Cloves

Ginger

Nutmeg

Bay

Spices and herbs were used in anti-freckle recipes

Opal

Drops from the deadly nightshade plant made the eyes sparkle

Mercury

Lemon

Lemon juice and poisonous mercury were used in face washes

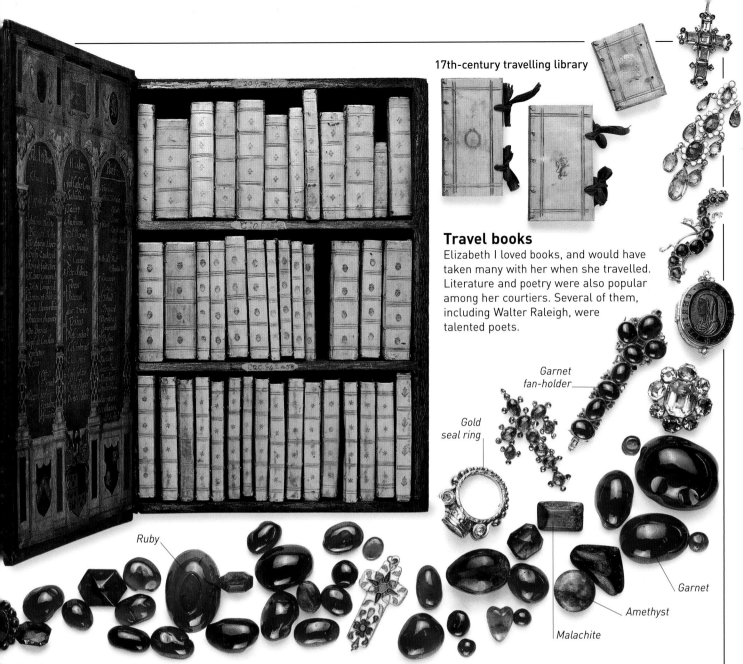

Travel books

Elizabeth I loved books, and would have taken many with her when she travelled. Literature and poetry were also popular among her courtiers. Several of them, including Walter Raleigh, were talented poets.

Garnet fan-holder

Gold seal ring

Ruby

Garnet

Amethyst

Malachite

Dripping with jewels

Both men and women at court competed to look as expensively dressed as possible. Courtiers spent lavishly on jewels, which they used to decorate every item of clothing from their shoes to their hats.

Signature of Elizabeth I

Signature of Robert Devereux, Earl of Essex

Pride comes before a fall

The Earl of Essex was one of the Queen's favourites. In 1601, he led a rebellion against the Queen, which failed, and Essex was beheaded. Shakespeare refers to the Earl's downfall in *Much Ado About Nothing.*

Royal procession

Elizabeth I's courtiers sometimes carried her through London in a seat called a palanquin. This gave ordinary people a chance to see their Queen. This 19th-century woodcut was copied from a 1601 painting by Robert Peake.

The playwrights

The London stage was dominated in the early 1590s by the plays of a group of university-educated men, such as Robert Greene, Christopher Marlowe, and Thomas Nashe. By 1592, Shakespeare was also an established playwright. His success was due partly to the fact that he was once a player – he knew what worked on stage and what did not.

Sweet revenge
Shakespeare learned to write by watching and acting in a new type of play called a "revenge tragedy", in which a murder is committed, then violently avenged. One of his first plays was the revenge tragedy *Titus Andronicus*.

The sloping surface allows the quill pen to be held at the right angle to the paper

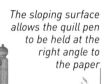

Oak leaf with gall

Making ink
Black ink was made from swellings called galls found on oak trees. The galls were crushed and mixed with water or vinegar and a chemical called green vitriol, made by pouring acid over rusty nails. The final ingredient was gum arabic, the dried sap of the acacia tree.

Rusty nails

17th-century inkwell and quills

Sitting comfortably
Before becoming a writer, the playwright Thomas Kyd worked as a scrivener, or copier of documents. He would have sat at a desk like this making neat copies of legal documents and plays. Most playwrights did not have special writing desks – they wrote wherever they could.

"Now, Faustus, let thine eyes with horror stare
Into that vast perpetual torture-house,
There are the furies tossing damned souls
On burning forks. Their bodies broil in lead."

CHRISTOPHER MARLOWE
EVIL ANGEL IN *DOCTOR FAUSTUS*

Tools of the trade

All educated people knew how to cut a pen from a goose feather using a penknife. Playwrights like Shakespeare had to keep their penknife close at hand, ready for when the quill's nib wore out and a new one needed to be cut.

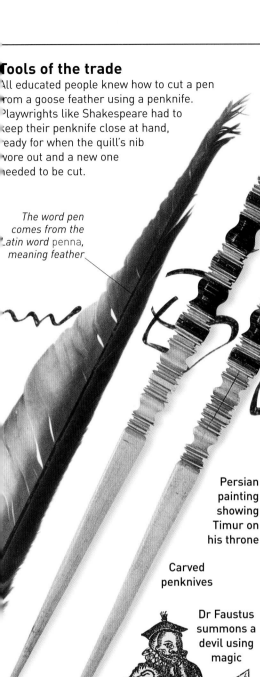

The word pen comes from the Latin word penna, *meaning feather*

Carved penknives

Last words

Just before his death in 1592, Robert Greene wrote an attack on Shakespeare calling him an "upstart crow". He looked down on Shakespeare because he had not gone to university.

William Shakespeare's signature

Rapid writing

Writing seemed to come easily to William Shakespeare. His fellow playwright Ben Jonson wrote that "Whatsoever he penned, he never blotted out a line."

Persian painting showing Timur on his throne

Dr Faustus summons a devil using magic

Marlowe

The writer who most influenced Shakespeare was Christopher Marlowe (1564–1593). Marlowe put stirring speeches into the mouths of tragic heroes such as Dr Faustus, a scholar who sells his soul to the devil.

Timur

Marlowe's first play *Tamburlaine* tells the story of Timur, a 14th-century Turkish warrior famous for his "conquering sword".

13

England at war

King of Spain
Philip II wanted to add England to his vast empire, and bring the country back into the Catholic faith.

From 1585 to 1604, Protestant England was at war with Catholic Spain, ruled by King Philip II. The war created a mood of patriotism in the country, and people wanted to see plays drawn from English history with battles on the stage. So, in the 1590s, Shakespeare wrote nine plays dealing with English history, featuring kings, wars, and battles for the throne.

Spanish galleons were taller than English ships, and harder to manoeuvre

God's winds
In 1588, a vast fleet of Spanish ships called the Armada was beaten in battle and scattered by storms. English people took this as a sign that God was on their side.

Henry IV comes to parliament to make his claim to the throne

Famous last words
The play *Richard II* tells how King Richard II was overthrown by his cousin, who became Henry IV. The play contains Shakespeare's famous patriotic speech, spoken by John of Gaunt: "This happy breed of men... this blessed plot, this earth, this realm, this England."

Sir John Falstaff
Falstaff is the drunken knight who befriends Prince Hal in the two *Henry IV* plays. The plays show a series of rebellions against Henry IV, whose troubled reign is God's punishment for overthrowing Richard II.

Agincourt
Henry V tells the story of England's great victory over the French at the Battle of Agincourt in 1415. "Follow your spirit," cries the King, "and cry God for Harry, England, and Saint George!"

Murder most foul

[I]n *Richard III*, Shakespeare [c]reated one of his most famous [vi]llains. Richard murders [h]is nephews in order [t]o become King [o]f England.

Linstocks from the wreck of the *Mary Rose*, which sank in 1545

Light my fire

Linstocks like these held lighted fuses for firing cannons on warships. By the 1580s, England had the most powerful warships in Europe. Real cannons were fired during the battle scenes in Shakespeare's history plays.

Elizabethan pipes and smoking accessories

Pipe smoking was introduced to England from North America

Model of a Spanish galleon

Each galleon bristled with cannons, which fired out through [o]penings called ports in the sides of the ship

Tobacco pouch and pipe

This pouch and pipe belonged to Sir Walter Ralegh, the joint leader of a daring raid on the Spanish port of Cadiz in 1596. Raleigh also founded the first English settlement in North America.

Earl of Essex

Traitor

The other hero of the 1596 raid on Cadiz was the Earl of Essex. In later years, both Raleigh and Essex were beheaded as traitors.

Enemies and protectors

The popularity of the theatre in London attracted hostility from powerful enemies. The Lord Mayor and his officials saw any large gathering as a threat to law and order, and were always trying to close down the playhouses. Fortunately, the actors were supported by the Queen and her courtiers, who loved to watch plays.

Powerful patrons

In 1594, the Lord Chamberlain, Henry Carey (1524–96), became the patron of Shakespeare's theatre company. Carey was the Queen's cousin and one of her closest advisors.

Whipped out of town

It was against the law to perform plays without the permission of a powerful noble. Players caught performing illegally were whipped out of town.

The public was used to seeing criminals being punished in the streets

A beggar is whipped out of town

Scandalous!

In 1597, Ben Jonson was put in prison for writing *The Isle of Dogs*, a play said to be "full of scandalous matter". This shows that, despite their noble protectors, playwrights could still get into trouble if they put on controversial plays.

Portrait of Ben Jonson (1572–1637)

Powerless protest

The Lord Mayor had no control over what went on outside the city walls, where most of the playhouses were built. All he could do was send letters of angry protest to the Queen's ministers.

Lord Mayor

Aldermen, members of the council

Puritans dressed more simply than other people

Puritans

The Puritans objected to the theatre because they thought that people should spend all their time in work or prayer.

Some gentlemen were so busy applauding the players on stage that they did not notice they were being robbed

Lessons in lifting

London was full of thieves called cutpurses, many of whom worked in gangs. In 1585, a school for boy cutpurses was discovered in Billingsgate, London. The boys were taught how to steal coins from a purse without ringing the bells that were attached to it.

Cutting a purse was called "nipping a bung" in criminal slang

The cutpurse waits for the right moment to cut the purse strings

A gentleman's well-cut clothes stood out in the yard, where the poorest members of the audience gathered, and were likely to attract the attention of a cutpurse

Trousers were worn tucked inside boots for riding

Boys made good cutpurses because they were small enough not to be noticed and had nimble fingers

Country gentleman

Visitors from outside London were less aware than city people of the risk of being robbed by a cutpurse. Robberies took place regularly in the playhouses. This provided the Lord Mayor with an argument for closing them, although he exaggerated the number of crimes committed.

Robbing place

Playhouses were ideal places for cutpurses because they were so crowded. Despite this, thieves were sometimes caught in the act and beaten up by angry members of the audience.

17

Jigs and jokes
Will Kemp was a popular comic actor in the Lord Chamberlain's Men. Kemp always danced a jig at the end of a show and in 1600, he danced from London to Norwich – a distance of more than 160 km (99.4 miles).

In 1594, Shakespeare joined a new company called the Lord Chamberlain's Men. He wrote about two plays a year for them and also worked as an actor. The company performed at the Theatre in London, which was owned by James Burbage. Shakespeare invested money in the company and, in return, took a share of the profits.

Sly swordsman
William Sly was a player in the Lord Chamberlain's Men. He was a skilled swordsman, and often played fiery young men like Hotspur in *Henry IV Part One* and Tybalt in *Romeo and Juliet*.

Many costumes were made from scratch by members of the company

The stage hand sweeps up after a show at the Theatre

Hired help
The job of the stage hands was to fire the canon, make sure that props were in the right place, clear up the rubbish, and operate the special effects.

Costumes and props were kept in baskets when not in use

Richard's rival

Edward Alleyn (1566–1626) was the star of the Lord Admiral's Men, and Richard Burbage's only real rival. He made his name playing Marlowe's heroes Dr Faustus and Tamburlaine.

Tragic transformation

Shakespeare wrote his greatest tragic roles for James Burbage's son, Richard (1568–1619). Richard was famous for completely transforming himself into a character.

Dress, to be worn by a boy player playing a woman

Tireman admiring a new wig

Costume care

The tireman was in charge of the costumes. Some of the costumes were bought from London tailors, while others were made by the company.

Work table, where costumes were made and altered to suit new roles

Behind the scenes

This room in the modern Globe Theatre in London is designed to show visitors what a tiring, or dressing, room would have looked like in Shakespeare's day. Costumes, wigs, and props were all stored in the tiring room.

Building the Globe

In 1597, the Theatre was forced to close. It had been built on rented land and the lease had come to an end. In December 1598, the Burbage brothers hired workmen to pull the Theatre down. They took the oak timbers by boat to Bankside, where they used them to build a new playhouse called the Globe.

The Globe's stage, as imagined by George Cruikshank in 1863

Round pegs and joints

Square pegs and joints

Knock down
The wooden joints of the Theatre were fixed with pegs. The workmen could knock them apart with hammers and use the undamaged timbers to make the new frame.

Wall story
After making the frame, the builders fitted wall panels. These were made from wattle (woven mats of hazel stems) covered with daub (a mixture of clay, lime, straw, horsehair, and dung).

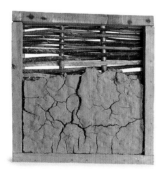

Interior decor
Special tools were used to carve and chisel the decorative features. The interior was colourful, with the stage columns painted to look like marble.

Awls for making small holes

Billhook for pruning and lopping

Auger for boring holes in wood

Hammer

Broad axe

Hand saw

Chisel

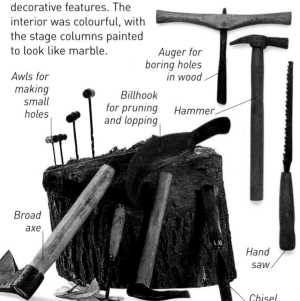

Gentlemen's room for wealthy spectators

Gallery seats

Hell (space beneath the stage)

Model theatre

This model gives us an idea of how the Globe may have looked. It is based on a 1596 sketch of the Swan playhouse. Excavations in 1989 revealed that the Globe was 30 m (99 ft) wide.

Stamp showing the Globe (the theatre actually had 20 sides)

Pole for the playhouse flag

Upper rooms, where cannons were fired as a sound effect

Flying the flag

Each playhouse had its own flag, flown on the days of a performance. The Globe also had a sign above its entrance, showing Hercules carrying a globe.

The **Rose**

The **Swan**

The **Globe**

To tile or not to tile?

The roof of the Globe was made of layers of straw and reeds. Thatched roofs were far cheaper than tiled roofs, but they were also a fire risk.

Thatched roof shielded the galleries from the weather

In a play, the balcony could represent castle battlements or an upper window

Heavens (stage roof) – the underside was painted to look like a starry sky

Two columns held up the heavens

Stage stuck out into the yard, where the poorest people stood to watch the plays

Staging a play

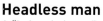
Morion, a type of Spanish helmet

Plays at the Globe were performed in the afternoons, by daylight. The scenery was limited, but there were some wonderful special effects. Angels and gods were lowered from the "heavens", and devils and ghosts came up through a trapdoor on stage. At the back of the stage, there was a curtained-off area used for showing picture-like scenes, such as characters lying dead or asleep.

Swan stage
In 1596, a Dutch visitor named Johannes de Witt sketched the Swan playhouse, giving us the only image from that time of a Shakespearean stage. It is bare apart from a bench. The scene might be set anywhere, from a palace to a ship's deck.

Rapier was used for fencing

Dagger was used in the left hand

The belt had a scabbard, where the rapier was kep[t]

Playing at soldiers
When players rushed on stage in full armour, waving swords, the audience knew that they were watching a battle. If the players carried scaling ladders, as in *Henry V*, the battle would become a siege.

Play plot
The "platt", or plot, of a play was posted backstage. It listed the scenes, with the exits and entrances of all the characters. The actors needed to refer to the platt because they had not read the whole play. Each player was given only his own part to learn.

Platt from The Seven Deadly Sins, Part Two

Headless man
A "beheaded man" could be shown on stage using two actors and a special table. The audience would see the "headless" body of a man, with his head apparently displayed at his feet.

Spilt blood
Pigs' or sheeps' blood was often used in scenes of violent death. In one play, a character had a fake head cut off. The head contained a pig's bladder, filled with blood, which gushed all over the stage.

"Our statues and our images of Gods... Our giants, monsters, furies, beasts and bugbears, Our helmets, shields, and vizors, hairs and beards, Our pasteboard marchpanes and our wooden pies..."

RICHARD BROME
LIST OF PLAYHOUSE PROPERTIES IN *THE ANTIPODES*

Grave trouble

The trapdoor allowed players to disappear and appear suddenly. The hole in the floor was also used to represent a grave. In this scene from a modern production of *Hamlet*, the trapdoor represents the grave of Ophelia.

Skull, a prop used in *Hamlet*

Useful props

Props helped to set the scene. Crowns were important props in the history plays. Skulls were used when actors were talking about death, and candles carried on to the stage told the audience that it was night.

Crown

Candle, often carried by a player dressed in a nightgown

The player puts his head through a hole in the table

Ruff was placed around the player's neck once his head was through the hole

The table surrounded by a curtain to hide what is underneath

The actor had to be careful not to blink or move

Music and dance

From the royal court to the peasant's cottage, music could be heard everywhere in Shakespeare's time. Many people played instruments, and Elizabethan audiences expected to hear good music when they went to the theatre. In Shakespeare's plays, there are more than 300 stage directions calling for music. He also wrote more than 70 songs for his characters to sing.

A boy plays a viol to accompany a lively dance, late 1500s

A spring in your step

Many different dances were popular in Shakespeare's day. The galliard was a lively court dance with leaps, kicks, and springing steps, while the pavane was more stately. Ordinary people enjoyed less formal dances, such as the wild morris, danced with bells strapped to the legs.

Orpharian

This instrument was invented in 1580 by London instrument maker John Rose. He named it after Orpheus, a mythical ancient Greek musician.

Wire strings

Elaborately carved walnut body, inset with pearls and rubies

16th-century orpharian

Triangle *Lute*

Couple dancing the galliard, by Flemish artist Hieronymus Francken the Elder, 1540–1610

Serenade in front of Silvia's window, by John Gilbert, c. 1860

Love song

In *The Two Gentlemen of Verona*, Thurio, who is in love with Silvia, hires musicians to "give some evening music to her ear". Music performed to win a woman's love is known as a serenade.

Sounds for clowns

The pipe and tabor (drum) were played at the same time by one person. They were used to accompany jigs – the clowns' dances at the end of a performance.

Pipe

Mysterious melodies

The hautboy, or shawm, made an eerie, solemn sound, which Shakespeare used to create an atmosphere of dread in his tragedies.

A woodwind instrument, like an oboe

16th-century engraving by Crispin de Passe

Hautboy

Pipes produced a single continuous note called a drone

Second drone pipe

Lovers' lutes

A man often played the lute to win over the woman he loved. However, in *The Taming of the Shrew*, hot-tempered Katherina smashes Petruchio over the head with his lute!

Viol

Played with a bow, the viol was used to accompany dances. In *Twelfth Night*, the foolish Sir Andrew Aguecheek "plays o' the viol-de-gamboys" in order to appear fashionable.

Mouthpiece

Bagpipe blues

The bagpipe was mostly played at country dances. Falstaff, in *Henry IV Part One*, says that he feels as sad as "the drone of a Lincolnshire bagpipe".

Viol made in the 1600s

Bag was made of leather

The tune was played with the fingers on this pipe

Bagpipe

"Let the sounds of music creep in our ears."

WILLIAM SHAKESPEARE
LORENZO IN
THE MERCHANT OF VENICE

Classic lute

The sheep's gut strings were plucked with the fingers and thumb

Soothing sounds

Many people believed that soothing lute music had the ability to heal. In *King Lear*, the mad king is brought to his senses with music – almost certainly played on a lute.

Clothes and costumes

Players in Shakespeare's day always dressed in clothes of their own time. The wealthy paraded around in elaborate outfits that were padded to create startling shapes. There were strict laws about clothes, which were worn as a sign of rank. Players were the only people allowed to break these laws, when they dressed up as nobles on stage.

Leather and satin gloves

Sweet gloves
Fashionable ladies wore scented gloves. In *Much Ado About Nothing*, Hero says, "These gloves... are an excellent perfume."

17th-century diamond and amethyst necklace

Covered in jewels
Ladies covered themselves with items of jewellery, and had diamonds and pearls sewn into their dresses and hair. The boy players wore cheaper costume jewellery made from glass.

Sleeves stuffed with bombast, or horsehair

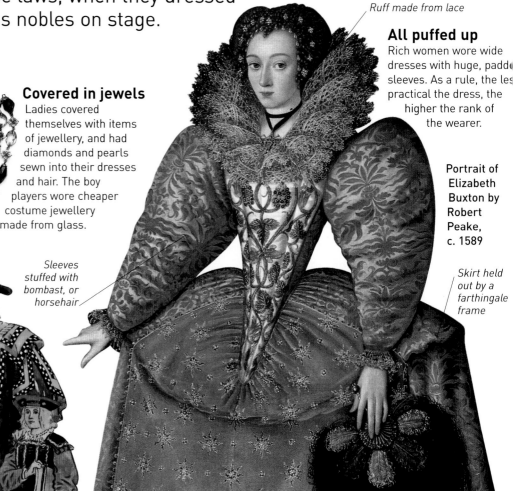

Ruff made from lace

All puffed up
Rich women wore wide dresses with huge, padded sleeves. As a rule, the less practical the dress, the higher the rank of the wearer.

Portrait of Elizabeth Buxton by Robert Peake, c. 1589

Skirt held out by a farthingale frame

Fashions for the stage
Modern productions of Shakespeare's plays use clothes from many different periods of history. These 1920s designs for *As You Like It* are early 1500s in style. Other productions have been set in Victorian, Elizabethan, or modern times.

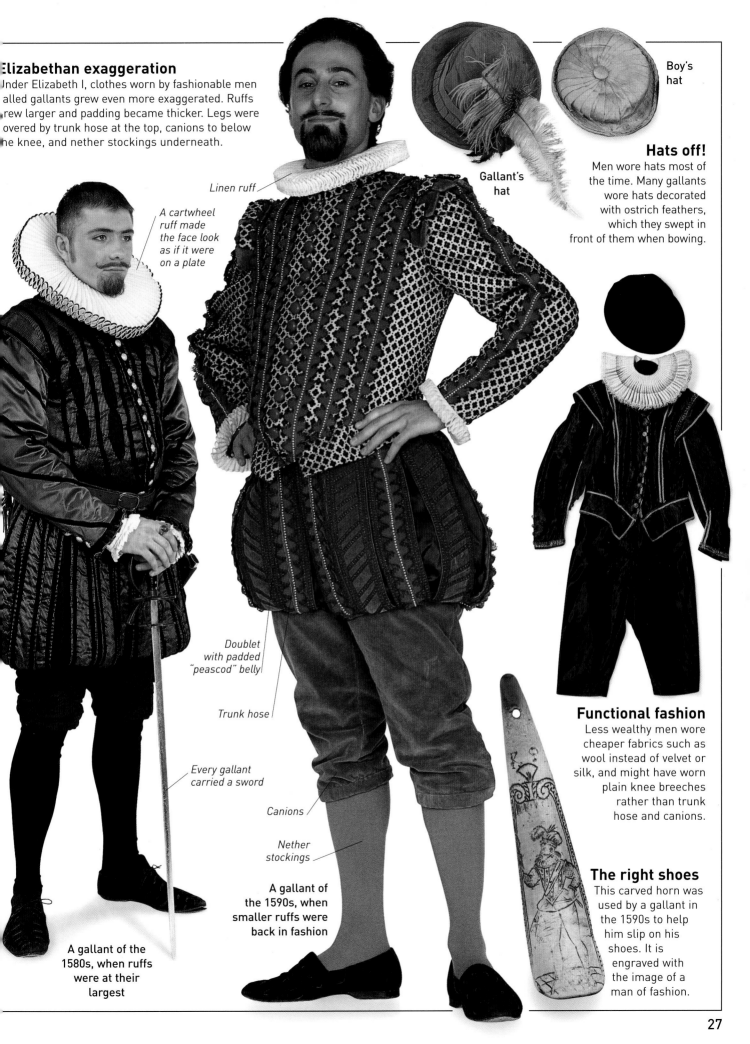

Elizabethan exaggeration

Under Elizabeth I, clothes worn by fashionable men called gallants grew even more exaggerated. Ruffs grew larger and padding became thicker. Legs were covered by trunk hose at the top, canions to below the knee, and nether stockings underneath.

Gallant's hat

Boy's hat

Hats off!

Men wore hats most of the time. Many gallants wore hats decorated with ostrich feathers, which they swept in front of them when bowing.

Linen ruff

A cartwheel ruff made the face look as if it were on a plate

Doublet with padded "peascod" belly

Trunk hose

Every gallant carried a sword

Canions

Nether stockings

A gallant of the 1590s, when smaller ruffs were back in fashion

A gallant of the 1580s, when ruffs were at their largest

Functional fashion

Less wealthy men wore cheaper fabrics such as wool instead of velvet or silk, and might have worn plain knee breeches rather than trunk hose and canions.

The right shoes

This carved horn was used by a gallant in the 1590s to help him slip on his shoes. It is engraved with the image of a man of fashion.

The boy player

In Shakespeare's time, only men could act on the English stage, so women's roles were performed by boys. Although these actors were called boy players, they probably played females until they were in their 20s. Shakespeare often had fun making the boy players act the parts of women disguised as men. For example, in the play *As You Like It*, the heroine Rosalind pretends to be a man called Ganymede.

Woman in disguise

In the film *Shakespeare in Love*, Gwyneth Paltrow plays a woman who disguises herself as a boy because she wants to go on stage.

The skirt is lowered over the farthingale

4 Skirt over hoop
He puts on an embroidered skirt, which will show through the front of the dress.

Wheel, or French, farthingale

Tireman

Pulling the laces tight will give the boy a waist

3 Outstanding!
The boy steps into a hooped farthingale that makes the skirt of the dress stand out.

2 Laced up
Next, he puts on a tight upper garment called a bodice. The tireman helps to lace up the back.

The petticoat protects the skin from the stiff fabric of the rest of the costume

1 Getting started
The boy player is getting ready to play Rosalind, the heroine of *As You Like It*. He starts by putting on a petticoat.

Fashionable figures
The fashion for exaggerated hips and bottoms was achieved with a farthingale – a series of hoops made of whalebone, wood, or wire – or a padded belt called a bum roll.

Bum roll

Wheel farthingale

Bell-shaped farthingale

The real thing
A boy player needed the help of the tireman to get ready for his performance. Once a boy was wearing his dress, make-up, and wig, he was totally convincing as a female. English travellers in Europe were always amazed to see real women acting there.

"If I were a woman I would kiss as many of you as had beards that pleased me."

WILLIAM SHAKESPEARE
ROSALIND IN *AS YOU LIKE IT*

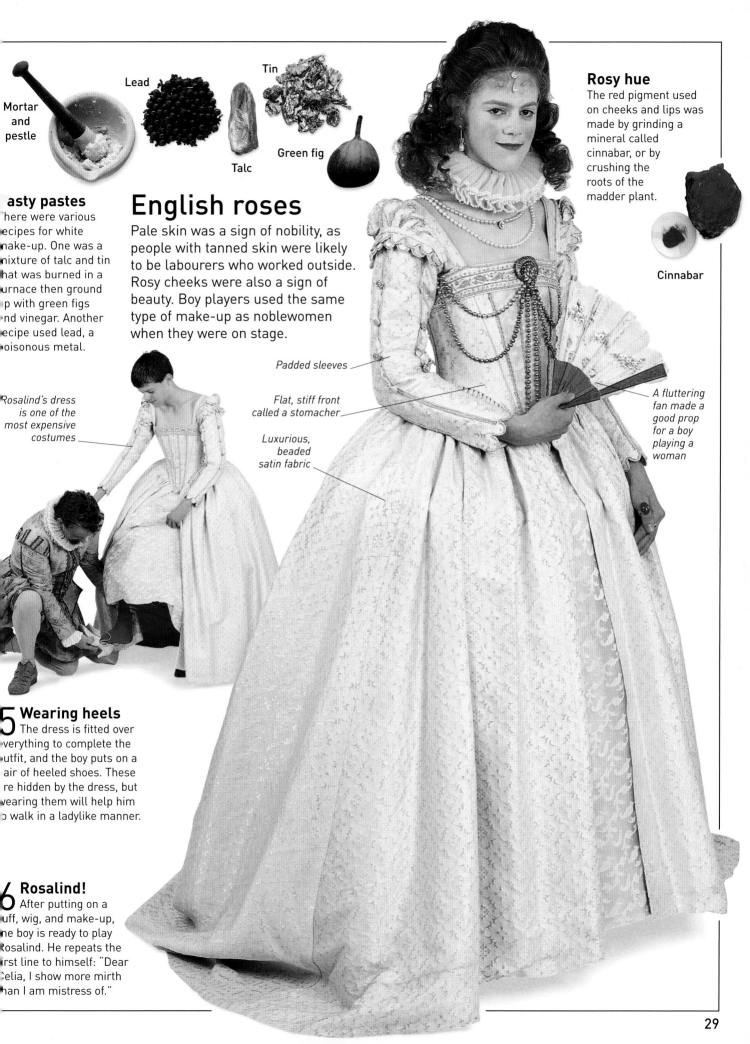

Mortar and pestle

Lead

Tin

Talc

Green fig

Nasty pastes

There were various recipes for white make-up. One was a mixture of talc and tin that was burned in a furnace then ground up with green figs and vinegar. Another recipe used lead, a poisonous metal.

English roses

Pale skin was a sign of nobility, as people with tanned skin were likely to be labourers who worked outside. Rosy cheeks were also a sign of beauty. Boy players used the same type of make-up as noblewomen when they were on stage.

Rosy hue

The red pigment used on cheeks and lips was made by grinding a mineral called cinnabar, or by crushing the roots of the madder plant.

Cinnabar

Padded sleeves

Flat, stiff front called a stomacher

Luxurious, beaded satin fabric

A fluttering fan made a good prop for a boy playing a woman

Rosalind's dress is one of the most expensive costumes

5 Wearing heels

The dress is fitted over everything to complete the outfit, and the boy puts on a pair of heeled shoes. These are hidden by the dress, but wearing them will help him to walk in a ladylike manner.

6 Rosalind!

After putting on a ruff, wig, and make-up, the boy is ready to play Rosalind. He repeats the first line to himself: "Dear Celia, I show more mirth than I am mistress of."

The audience

Playgoing was a popular form of entertainment in the late 1500s. As many as 3,000 people would gather to watch a show. Farmers, sailors, and servants stood side by side in the crowded yard. Lawyers and merchants filled the gallery seats, while nobles sat in the gentlemen's rooms next to the stage.

In the gallery
In this early 1900s drawing of the Globe, the audience watches a performance of *Henry IV*.

The apple-wives found it hard to make a living if the playhouses were closed

Shakespearian snacks
Apples and pears were sold as snacks in the playhouses in Shakespeare's time. Different varieties were available at different times. The first apples to ripen were called "Juneaters" because they were ready for eating on 29 June, St John's Day.

Williams pears

Pippins, grown in orchards in Kent, were the most common variety of apple

Pippin apples

Apples were bought as gifts for noblewomen

Nut carpet
In 1988 and 1989, archaeologists found hazelnut shells in the yards of the Rose and Globe. The shells were mixed with ash and used as a floor covering to keep the yards dry in wet weather.

Apple-wives
Female fruit-sellers called apple-wives loved the large audiences they found at the playhouses. They wandered around the yard and the galleries carrying baskets of fruit to sell to hungry customers.

According to the accounts of some theatregoers, groundlings stank of garlic and onions

Garlic cloves

The groundlings often heckled the players, shouting rude comments and throwing apples if they got bored

Money was carried in a purse dangling from a belt because few clothes at the time had pockets

Tankards were usually made from pewter or wood

Scarecrows

The people who stood in the yard were nicknamed "groundlings" or "scarecrows" because of their shabby appearance. They were also called "stinkards" because of the way they smelled.

Thieves

Playgoers risked being robbed by a cutpurse. Some thieves dressed as gentlemen and worked in the galleries, where the richest pickings were to be found.

Crowds of stinkards would sometimes start fights and riots – even the actors on the stage were not safe when they went on the rampage

Getting merry

Groundlings guzzled ale from tankards, while gallery folk preferred wine. Many of Shakespeare's characters, such as Sir John Falstaff in *The Merry Wives of Windsor*, drink a strong Spanish wine called sack.

"Your stinkard has the self-same liberty to be there in his tobacco fumes which your sweet courtier hath."

THOMAS DEKKER
THE GULL'S HORNBOOK, 1609

Comfort costs

It cost one penny to stand in the yard. For an extra penny, playgoers could sit in the gallery.

Coin found at the Rose playhouse

Shakespeare's comedies

In Shakespeare's time, a comedy meant simply a light-hearted play with a happy ending. In the 1590s, Shakespeare wrote ten comedies, most of them with plots taken from old love stories. He liked stories in which young lovers overcome various obstacles before being allowed to marry. The lovers might have to put on a disguise or run away from home. But everything always turns out all right in the end.

Shylock

Portia

Pound of flesh

In *The Merchant of Venice*, Shylock, a money-lender, claims that Antonio owes him a pound of flesh for failing to repay a debt. Portia, the heroine, disguises herself as a lawyer to defend Antonio.

Forest of Arden

When Rosalind, the heroine of *As You Like It*, is banished from court, she goes to live in the Forest of Arden. Jaques, a miserable lord, is also banished to the forest, where he meets Touchstone, a jester who shares his upside-down view of the world.

Jaques

Touchstone

Love and marriage

Although people were fascinated by love stories, in real life they rarely married for love. The upper classes usually married for money, or to improve their social rank.

When the locket is closed, the lovers are face to face

16th-century locket containing miniatures painted by Nicholas Hilliard

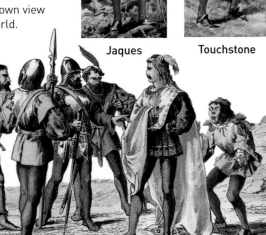

Valentine's day

Valentine, the hero of *The Two Gentlemen of Verona*, is exiled from Milan and captured by outlaws. The play ends with Valentine finding love and winning a pardon for his outlaw friends.

Ditched

In *The Merry Wives of Windsor*, Falstaff sends love letters to two "merry wives", hoping to get hold of their money. The wives find out and plot revenge. In one scene, Falstaff hides in a basket of dirty laundry and is then dumped in a ditch.

Malvolio is usually stern and cold, so, when he smiles continuously at Olivia, she thinks that he has gone mad

Magic and mischief

In *A Midsummer Night's Dream*, King Oberon asks Puck to drop a love potion in Queen Titania's eyes as she sleeps. On waking, she falls instantly in love with Bottom, the weaver. To cause mischief, Puck has given Bottom the head of an ass.

Bottom with the head of an ass

Malvolio dreams of being made Count Malvolio

Oberon cures Titania with a herb, thought to be wormwood

Wormwood (*Artemesia absinthium*)

Malvolio's name means "bad will"

Malvolio's costume is usually made as farcical as possible for the scene with Olivia

MARY PICKFORD & DOUGLAS FAIRBANKS in

ALL TALKING "TAMING OF THE SHREW" ALL LAUGHING

UNITED ARTISTS PICTURE

Making a good wife

This poster is for the 1929 film of *The Taming of the Shrew*. Petruchio, the hero, decides to marry bad-tempered Katherina for money, not love. The play shows how Petruchio goes about "taming" Katherina, turning her into an obedient wife.

Petruchio

Mad love

In *Twelfth Night*, Malvolio, the conceited steward of Olivia, receives a letter that he thinks is from Olivia. It says that she loves him, and tells him to wear yellow stockings and to smile at her. Malvolio follows the orders and ends up being locked up as a madman.

Olivia has sworn to wear a veil for seven years, mourning her dead brother

Olivia

Malvolio, the central character of the comic sub-plot in *Twelfth Night*

"And each several chamber bless Through this palace with sweet peace; And the owner of it blessed Ever shall in safety rest."

WILLIAM SHAKESPEARE
OBERON IN *A MIDSUMMER NIGHT'S DREAM*

The King's Men

Queen Elizabeth I died on 24 March 1603 and the crown passed to her closest male relative, James VI of Scotland. He was crowned James I of England on 25 July 1603, founding the Stuart dynasty. James was a supporter of the theatre, and became the patron of Shakespeare's company, which was renamed the King's Men. To please the King, Shakespeare wrote *Macbeth*, a tragedy with a Scottish setting.

Coat-of-arms
One sign of Shakespeare's growing success was that in 1596 he received a coat-of-arms, the badge of a gentleman.

James I of England
James I (1566–1625) was crowned in 1603, but was unable to come to London until 15 March 1604. He was kept away by a terrible new outbreak of the plague.

Royal touch
These gold "touchpieces" were given by James I to people suffering from a disease called scrofula. A royal touch was supposed to cure the disease.

Noble frog
In the early 1600s, it was fashionable for courtiers to carry purses in the shape of unusual objects or animals, such as this frog. Although frogs were linked with witchcraft in *Macbeth*, they were also a symbol of spring.

The ghost of Banquo makes a terrifying appearance at a feast

Macbeth cries, "Hence, horrible shadow!" when he sees Banquo's ghost

Crow

Toad

Evil spirits
Witches were thought to have evil spirit helpers, which took the shape of animals such as black cats, toads, and crows. In the 17th century, hundreds of innocent people were accused of witchcraft.

Black cat

Murder and treason
In *Macbeth*, the witches tell Macbeth that he will be King of Scotland, but that his friend Banquo will be the father of Kings. Macbeth murders the King to seize the crown, then kills Banquo

Curse of *Macbeth*

The black magic in *Macbeth* has led to a belief among superstitious actors that the play is cursed. According to the 17th-century writer John Aubrey, bad luck followed the play from its first performance, when the boy playing Lady Macbeth fell sick and died. Actors try to beat the curse by never mentioning the play's title, calling it "the Scottish play" instead.

This witch's costume was used in a Royal Shakespeare production of Macbeth

Actors say it is bad luck to wear costumes from Macbeth *in any other production*

Achilles drags Hector's body behind his chariot

Hector's horrified parents watch from Troy

Comedy or tragedy?

This Roman lamp shows a scene from the Trojan war, the subject of Shakespeare's *Troilus and Cressida*, one of three plays that are difficult to categorize. *All's Well That Ends Well*, *Measure for Measure*, and *Troilus and Cressida* share many features of comedy, but they are also dark and gloomy in mood.

The dark colours of the costume reflect the description by Shakespeare of the ugly "midnight hags"

Dress made of torn strips of cotton

Family feud

Romeo and Juliet tells the story of two young lovers who are kept apart by a family feud. It takes the tragic deaths of the lovers to bring the feud to an end.

The famous tragedies

In the early 1600s, Shakespeare wrote the great tragedies *Hamlet*, *King Lear*, *Othello*, and *Macbeth*. These four plays contain Shakespeare's most famous poetry, and provided his star Richard Burbage with his greatest roles. The plays also contain exciting action scenes, such as the fencing duel at the end of *Hamlet*.

Hamlet thrusts at Laertes's right shoulder, scoring a hit

Laertes tries to stab Hamlet, who deflects the blow

Laertes defends himself against Hamlet

Laertes catches Hamlet off guard and cuts him with his poisoned sword – it will be his death blow

Hamlet is the better swordsman

Hamlet thrusts at Laertes's thigh

Fighting fit

Players had to be skilled at swordfighting. Gentlemen learned fencing as part of their education, so, if they saw clumsy fighting in a play, they would boo the players off the stage.

Deadly duel

Hamlet does not know that the villain Claudius has persuaded Laertes to use a poisoned sword. In the duel, both Laertes and Hamlet are wounded by the sword. The dying Laertes confesses to Hamlet, who kills Claudius before he dies himself.

Street fight

Shakespeare wrote swordfights into several of his plays. In *Romeo and Juliet* Romeo's friend Mercutio fights Juliet's cousin Tybalt in a street brawl

OTHELLO

Tricked
The hero of *Othello* is a Moor (North African) married to Desdemona. The evil villain, Iago, plots Othello's downfall by making him suspect that Desdemona is unfaithful. Driven mad by jealousy, Othello murders his innocent wife. Too late, he realizes that he has made a mistake.

Iago

Othello

This poster, advertising a production of *Othello*, shows the Moor preparing to kill his sleeping wife Desdemona

Fencers used a light, thin stabbing sword called a rapier

Hamlet gazes at his father's ghost, but his mother Gertrude cannot see the ghost, and thinks that her son is mad

Foolish father
In *King Lear*, an old king divides his kingdom between two wicked daughters and rejects the daughter who loves him. He eventually comes to understand how foolish he has been.

Most unnatural murder
In the 1947 film *Hamlet*, Laurence Olivier played the Danish prince. He is ordered by the ghost of his father to avenge his "foul and most unnatural murder".

Hamlet is the most complex of Shakespeare's heroes

Polonius, Laertes's father, is accidentally killed by Hamlet, who mistakes him for the King

*"So shall you hear
Of carnal, bloody,
and unnatural acts,
Of accidental judgements,
casual slaughters."*

WILLIAM SHAKESPEARE
HORATIO IN *HAMLET*

The Roman plays

In the early 1600s, both Shakespeare and Ben Jonson wrote tragedies set in ancient Rome. This subject was familiar to educated members of their audiences, thanks to the influence of Roman writers such as Seneca. Setting plays in Rome allowed playwrights to discuss political issues without risking offending the government.

Poster for a 1965 production of *Coriolanus*

Roman reject

In *Coriolanus*, Shakespeare tells the story of an ambitious Roman nobleman called Coriolanus, who is a great warrior but a poor politician. When the people of Rome reject Coriolanus, he joins the city's enemies, the Volscians.

In the play Julius Caesar, *the ghost of the murdered leader returns to speak to Brutus, the man who killed him*

Offending portrait

Julius Caesar (100–44 BCE) was the subject of Shakespeare's first Roman play. Caesar was a Roman general, who was murdered because he started to act like a king. He was the first Roman to put his portrait on a coin, which offended many people.

Roman coin with the portrait of Julius Caesar

Brutus asks the ghost if he is "some devil that mak'st my blood turn cold and my hair to stare"

Brutus, who plans Caesar's murder

Mark Antony, who defeats Brutus in war

Murdering hero

The hero of *Julius Caesar* is Caesar's friend and killer, Brutus. After Caesar's murder, Mark Antony rouses the people of Rome with his famous speech, "Friends, Romans, countrymen, lend me your ears."

The folds of togas make good places for actors playing the killers in Julius Caesar to hide their daggers

Cobra, the type of snake with which Cleopatra may have killed herself

Cleopatra with her maid Charmian

1940s US actress Katherine Cornell as Cleopatra

In ancient Rome, purple was a sign of high rank

Love before duty

In *Antony and Cleopatra*, Antony falls in love with Cleopatra, the Queen of Egypt. Lovestruck, Antony forgets his duties to Rome. The play ends with the suicide of the lovers. Antony stabs himself and Cleopatra makes a deadly snake bite her.

Togas or cloaks?

Roman citizens dressed in elaborately folded robes called togas. But Shakespeare would not have known what a toga was. The Roman characters in his plays would have worn cloaks, as courtiers did in Shakespeare's time.

Squeaking Cleopatra

Miss Darragh played Cleopatra to Jerrold Robertshaw's Antony in this 20th-century production. Witty and clever, Cleopatra dies imagining her story being performed on stage, with a "squeaking" boy playing her role.

The romances

In 1608, the King's Men took over a second playhouse at Blackfriars. The new audience, made up of wealthy Londoners, inspired a new style of playwriting. Between 1608 and 1611, Shakespeare wrote four plays for the Blackfriars. Known as the romances, they have in common fairytale plots, the adventures of noble heroes and heroines, and families broken apart and reunited.

Regret and reunion
This photo is from a 1966 production of *A Winter's Tale*. King Leontes thinks that Polixenes is in love with his wife and locks her away. After she fakes her own death, the royal couple are reunited.

Shipwreck spell
The Tempest tells the story of Prospero, a magician living on an island with a band of fairy spirits. He uses magic to wreck a ship carrying his enemies.

Novel idea
Shakespeare was inspired by stories such as *Arcadia* by Sir Philip Sydney (1593). It tells the tale of two disguised princes in their search for love.

Stage romances
Shakespeare was also inspired by playwrights Francis Beaumont and John Fletcher, who had been writing stage romances since 1607. Fletcher later worked with Shakespeare on his last three plays.

Illustration for *The Tempest* by Robert Dudley, 1856

Prospero's spirits bring a banquet to the shipwrecked seafarers

Illustration for *Cymbeline* by Robert Dudley, 1856

"... I come To answer thy best pleasure; be't to fly, To swim, to dive into the fire, to ride On the curled clouds..."

WILLIAM SHAKESPEARE
ARIEL IN *THE TEMPEST*

Plot twists
In the play *Cymbeline*, Posthumus and Imogen are forced to part when Posthumus is banished. *Cymbeline* has more plot twists than any other Shakespeare play, with eight surprises in a row in the final scene.

Miraculous music

Pericles tells the story of Thaisa, who is buried at sea by her grieving husband Pericles. She is washed ashore at Ephesus, where she is brought back to life by the miraculous power of music.

Chest holding Thaisa, found on the seashore

Illustration from *The Children's Shakespeare* (1911) by Charles Folkard

The playwright's signature

Part of the legal document giving Shakespeare the rights to the house at Blackfriars

New house

In 1613, Shakespeare bought a house close to the Blackfriars playhouse. He did not spend much time here as he had already gone back to live in Stratford.

Fancy dress

A type of court entertainment called a masque (a mixture of ballet, opera, and fancy dress) influenced the staging at the Blackfriars playhouse. In *The Tempest*, Prospero stages his own masque with the help of magic.

Woman in a masque costume, c. 1615

Return to Stratford

After finishing *The Tempest* in 1611, Shakespeare returned to Stratford. Now a wealthy man, he went to live in New Place, the house that he had bought for his family in 1597. Shakespeare died on 23 April 1616, and was buried at the Holy Trinity Church in Stratford with the words "Curst be he that moves my bones" inscribed on his grave.

Home study

Shakespeare continued to write for about two years after he returned to Stratford. He visited London from time to time to work with John Fletcher on the three plays *Henry VIII*, *Two Noble Kinsmen*, and a lost play called *Cardenio*.

Last lines

In 1613, Shakespeare wrote his last lines for the theatre in the play *Two Noble Kinsmen*. This little-known play tells the story of two friends, Palamon and Arcite. The characters, shown here in a production of the play at the modern Globe Theatre, both fall for the beautiful Emilia, and rivalry in love turns them into bitter enemies.

Sound effect backfires

On 29 June 1613, disaster struck at the Globe during a performance of *Henry VIII*. Sparks from the playhouse cannon set fire to the thatched roof and the Globe was burned to the ground. At about this time, Shakespeare retired from writing for good.

The cannon was fired to announce the arrival of the King, played by Richard Burbage

The Globe was rebuilt on the foundations of the building destroyed by fire

The Globe 1614

25

Elizabethan cannon with bronze barrel and reproduction wooden stand

Raised from the ashes

The King's Men rebuilt the Globe with a fireproof, tiled roof, and reopened it in 1614.

Hall Croft, Stratford

In 1607, Shakespeare's daughter Susanna went to live at Hall Croft with her new husband John Hall. Shakespeare approved of John and would have returned home for the wedding. During his last years in London, Shakespeare would have returned to Stratford for events such as his mother's funeral in 1608.

A good likeness

In 1623, a stone statue of Shakespeare, sculpted by Geerart Janssen, was installed in the Holy Trinity Church. The monument is likely to be an accurate portrait of the writer as it was approved by his family.

Will's will

Shakespeare left his houses and land to his eldest daughter Susanna. His younger daughter Judith received £300, a large sum at the time. Shakespeare's wife Anne received only his second-best bed, but it is likely that she remained at New Place until her death in 1623.

Mourning jewellery was often decorated with reminders of death such as skulls and skeletons

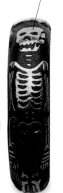

17th-century mourning ring

Remember me

Shakespeare also left money to his closest friends from the King's Men so that they could buy gold mourning rings in his memory.

Printed plays

17th-century image of a pressman laying out letters for printing

Shakespeare had little interest in seeing his plays in print. They were written to be performed, and could reach a far larger audience at the Globe than they would as books. About half of Shakespeare's plays were published during his lifetime, as little books called quartos. Seven years after his death, Shakespeare's plays were published in a single volume, known as the First Folio.

Hard pressed

Printing in Shakespeare's day was a slow process. Metal letters in a frame were placed on a "coffin" and inked with a ball. A pressman put the paper on a frame called a tympan, and lowered it onto the coffin. He then slid the coffin under a plate called a platen. Finally, he lowered the platen, pressing the paper onto the inky letters.

Heavy platen, or printing plate

Sturdy wooden frame

Hand press

Quarto

This edition of *A Midsummer Night's Dream* was printed in 1600. Each copy cost six pennies – six times the cost of seeing the play on stage. The name quarto, meaning fourth, comes from the fact that four pages were printed on each side of a single sheet.

First folio

In 1623, Henry Condell and John Heminges published 36 of Shakespeare's plays in the leather-bound First Folio. A folio (the Latin word for leaf) is a large book with pages made up of standard sheets, or leaves, of paper folded in half.

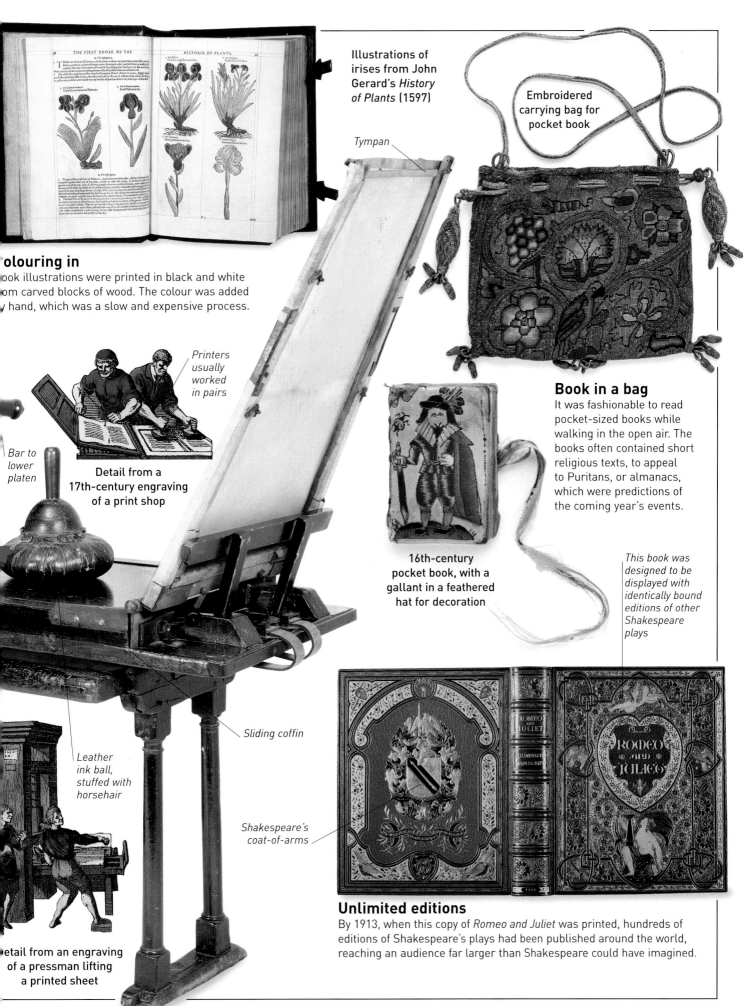

Illustrations of irises from John Gerard's *History of Plants* (1597)

Tympan

Embroidered carrying bag for pocket book

Colouring in

ook illustrations were printed in black and white om carved blocks of wood. The colour was added y hand, which was a slow and expensive process.

Printers usually worked in pairs

Detail from a 17th-century engraving of a print shop

Bar to lower platen

Book in a bag

It was fashionable to read pocket-sized books while walking in the open air. The books often contained short religious texts, to appeal to Puritans, or almanacs, which were predictions of the coming year's events.

16th-century pocket book, with a gallant in a feathered hat for decoration

This book was designed to be displayed with identically bound editions of other Shakespeare plays

Sliding coffin

Leather ink ball, stuffed with horsehair

Shakespeare's coat-of-arms

etail from an engraving of a pressman lifting a printed sheet

Unlimited editions

By 1913, when this copy of *Romeo and Juliet* was printed, hundreds of editions of Shakespeare's plays had been published around the world, reaching an audience far larger than Shakespeare could have imagined.

Shakespeare's legacy

"He was not of an age, but for all time," wrote the playwright Ben Jonson to describe his friend William Shakespeare, and he has been proved right. Shakespeare's plays are still performed all over the world and have inspired films, ballets, musicals, and operas. His other great legacy is to the English language. Hundreds of everyday words and phrases such as "cold-blooded" and "fair play" appeared first in a Shakespeare play.

Dreamy dish
Designed in 1853 by W B Kirk, this porcelain fruit bowl is decorated with a lively scene from *A Midsummer Night's Dream*.

Herbert Beerbohm Tree as Cardinal Wolsey in *Henry VIII*

Captured in glass
This stained-glass window depicting some of Shakespeare's comic characters is in Southwark Cathedral, London, where the playwright worshipped. The window, designed by Christopher Webb, was unveiled in 1954.

Cartoons
In the 1990s, some of Shakespeare's plays were made into cartoons for children's television. In this scene from *A Midsummer Night's Dream*, Oberon is about to wake Titania from a spell, saying, "Now my Titania; wake you, my sweet queen."

Spectacular Shakespeare
British actor-manager Herbert Beerbohm Tree was famous for his spectacular and lavish productions of Shakespeare's plays in the late 19th and early 20th centuries.

Stratford's market square hung with banners for the Shakespeare Jubilee in 1769

Stratford celebrations

Each year, millions of tourists visit Stratford to see where Shakespeare was born and raised. Tourists first came to Stratford in 1769, when actor and producer David Garrick organized the Shakespeare Jubilee.

Putting it to music

In the 1940s and '50s, two of Shakespeare's plays were turned into popular musicals – *Kiss Me Kate*, based on *The Taming of the Shrew*, and *West Side Story*, which is the tale of *Romeo and Juliet* set in New York. Operatic adaptations of Shakespeare's plays include Verdi's *Macbeth*, *Othello*, and *Falstaff*, all composed in the second half of the 19th century.

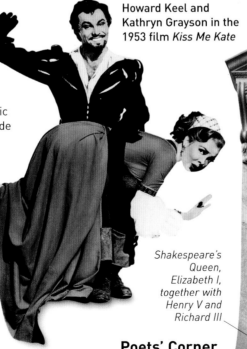

Howard Keel and Kathryn Grayson in the 1953 film *Kiss Me Kate*

Tempest in space

The 1956 film *Forbidden Planet* takes the story of Shakespeare's play *The Tempest* and sets it in outer space.

Shakespeare's Queen, Elizabeth I, together with Henry V and Richard III

Poets' Corner

In 1740, this statue of Shakespeare was set up in London's Westminster Abbey. It overlooks Poets' Corner, where some of Britain's greatest poets are buried or have memorials.

Index

Acknowledgements

Dorling Kindersley would like to thank:
Models: Kate Adams, Annabel Blackledge, Ken Brown, Nick Carter, David Evans, John Evans, James Halliwell, Jamie Hamblin, James Parkin, Alan Plank, Dan Rodway, and Johnny Wasylkiw. Make-up artists: Jordana Cox, Hayley Spicer. Props: Ken Brown. Wigs: Darren and Ronnie at The Wig Room. Armourer: Alan M. Meek. Stylist: Judy Hill. Costumes: The RSC, Stratford. Editorial assistance: Carey Scott. Index: Lynn Bresler. Wallchart: Steve Setford and Peter Radcliffe.

For this relaunch edition, the publisher would like to thank: Hazel Beynon for text editing and Carron Brown for proofreading.

The publishers would like to thank the following for their kind permission to reproduce their photographs:
a=above; b=below; c=centre; l=left; r=right; t=top

AKG London: 6tl, 11br, 24bl, 25tr, 32bl, 37tl, 40cla, 40cl, 40br, 41cra, 44tl, 45cl, 45bl, 47bc; British Library Add. Folio 57 Harley 1319 14cl; Erich Lessing 5clb, 24tl. Avoncroft Museum Historic Buildings: 20cl. Bridgeman Art Library: Beauchamp Collection, Devon 15br; Belvoir Castle; Bristol City Museum and Art Gallery, UK 41c; British Library 13br, 16bc, 44c; Christie's Images 45br; Dulwich Picture Gallery, London, UK 18c; Dyson Perrins Museum, Worcestershire, UK 46tl; Guildhall Library, Corporation of London, UK 41cl; Helmingham Hall, Suffolk, UK/Mark Fiennes 24cr; Linnean Society, London, UK 45tl; National Museums of Scotland 4b; Norfolk Museums Service (Norwich Castle Museum) UK 26br; Private Collection 16c, 22tl, 32cr, 40cr; Private Collection/Barbara Singer 15tl; Private Collection/Christie's Images 6tr; Private Collection/Ken Walsh 12–13; Private Collection/ The Stapleton Collection: 11bl; Victoria & Albert Museum, London, UK 6r, 26bl; Walker Art

Gallery Board of Trustees National Museums & Galleries on Merseyside 10c; Yale Center for British Art, Paul Mellon Fund, USA 20tr, 32br. British Library: 8–9, 11tl, 45tr, 45cr. © The British Museum: 11(main image), 8tl, 9tr, 35br, 38c. Robert Estall 6c. Photographic Survey Courtauld Institute of Art: Private Collection 16tl. By permission of the Trustees of Dulwich Picture Gallery: 19tc (detail). Dulwich College: 22cl. Mary Evans Picture Library: 4tl, 5cb, 7bl, 7bc, 9tl, 10tl, 13tr, 16cb, 16br, 18tl, 19tl, 34tl, 34tr, 34br, 40crr, 47t; Charles Folkard 41tl; ILN1910 30tl. Ronald Grant Archive: 33cr, 38tl, 38br, 39tc, 39br, 46cl, Animated Tales of Shakespeare's A Midsummer Night's Dream © BBC 46c; The Winter's Tale 1966 © Cressida Film Productions 40tl, Forbidden Planet © MGM 47bl; Hamlet 1948 © Two Cities 37cl. Mary Rose Trust: 15tc, 31cr. Museum of London Archaeology Service: Andy Chopping 31br. Courtesy of the Museum of London: 6bcl, 9bc, 10–11, 12br, 13tc, 20clb, 26cl, 34cl, 43br. National Maritime Museum, London: 14–15, 42bc. The Natural History Museum, London: 23tr. Post Office Picture Library: Shakespeare's Theatre Postage Stamps © The Post Office 1995. Reproduced by kind permission of The Post Office. All Rights Reserved 21tcl, 21tcr, 42br. Premier Brands: 14bl, 14br, 36tl, 36crb, 37tr, 37cr, 37bl, 37bll. Public Record Office: 43cl. The Royal College of Music, London: Division viol by Barak Norman, London, 1692 25tl. St Bride Printing Library: 44–45. Science Museum: 34cl. Shakespeare Birthplace Trust, Stratford-upon-Avon: 2cl, 2br, 2–3, 3br; Malcolm Davies 44cl; By kind permission of Jarrold Publishing 2tl, 42tl, 43tl. Shakespeare's Globe: Donald Cooper 42cr; Nik Milner 18–19; John Tramper 23tl. Courtesy of the Trustees of the V&A Picture Library: 2bl, 26tl. Vin Mag Archive: SAC 28tl. The Wallace Collection: 14tl, 15tr. Warwick Castle: 22tr. Weald and Downland Open Air Museum: 3tr. York Archaeology Trust: 12cl.

All other images © Dorling Kindersley.

For further information see:
www.dkimages.com